Bear Grylls

SURVIVAL SKILLS HANDBOOK

KNOTS

Bear Grylls

This survival handbook has been specially put together to help young adventurers just like you to stay safe in the wild. People have used the knots included in this book for years and they are just as valuable today. Early uses included making shelters, weaving, fishing, and tethering animals. Although they can take a while to master, the moment you tie a tricky knot and get to use it in action, you realize how exciting this ancient art can be!

Bear

CONTENTS

DISCOVER KNOTS!

A sound knowledge of ropes and knots is extremely important for climbers and mountaineers, but they also have uses in everyday life. It takes time and practice to master the art of knot tying, but it is very rewarding to put your skills to use!

Types of rope

Static ropes do not stretch, while dynamic ropes allow some movement if the load they are holding suddenly falls.

Laid rope

This rope is used in many outdoor activities. It has three or more strands twisted around each other.

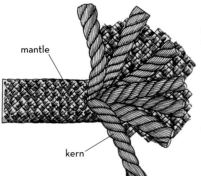

individual fibres make up each strand

mantle

kern

Kernmantle rope

Many climbing ropes have a protective sheath, called a mantle, covering the core fibres (kern).

Damaged ropes

The sheath of kernmantle ropes can hide a damaged core. Bulges in the core or tears in the mantle mean that the rope needs to be replaced.

damaged core

damaged mantle

Learn the terms

Turn	The U-shape that is formed when a rope is hung over a rail.
Round turn	A round turn is created when a rope is hung over a rail, and then wound around the rail one more time.
Half hitch	This knot is made when a rope is hung over a rail, then either under, or both under and over, itself.
Clove hitch	Two half hitches that are connected and placed next to each other make a clove hitch.
Standing end	The standing end, or standing part, refers to the main body of the rope.
Overhand turn	A circular shape in the rope where the working end finishes on top of the circle.
Underhand	A circular loop in the rope where the working end sits on the underside.
Working end	The portion of rope, other than the standing part, that is used to tie a knot. When the knot is finished, the working end is usually the small tail left over.
Bight	A bight is a U-shaped form made in the rope as part of the knot-tying process.

Carrying ropes

1 Put the two rope ends together. Measure out two armlengths, then loop the rest of the rope in double armlengths over your knee or around your shoulders. This is the main section that will sit on your back.

these two ends will become the shoulder straps

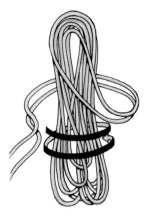

3 Pass a bight of rope through the top of the looped rope.

2 Wrap the two long ends tightly around the whole coil several times.

4 Run the loose ends through the bight of rope.

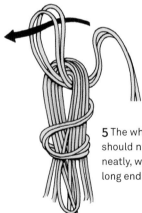

5 The whole rope should now hang neatly, with two long ends.

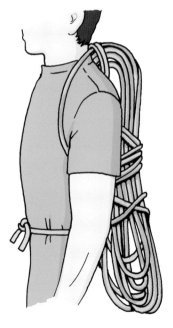

6 Run the long ends over your shoulders, then across your back, and tie across your stomach.

OVERHAND LOOP

One of the quickest ways to make a fixed loop in a rope is the overhand loop, suitable for a quick secure on a belay station. This knot can become very tight, however, and can be difficult to undo, so it isn't always the best choice.

> Loop knots are closed bights that have been tied either in the bight itself, or at the end of the rope.

1 Put the two rope ends together. Stretch the loop out over the top of the trailing rope.

loop follows the direction of the arrow

trailing rope

2 Pull the loop through the hole.

3 Attach the loop to a carabiner (metal loop, with a spring-loaded opening).

BEAR SAYS

This knot is suitable for a quick secure on a belay station (the point on the rope from which a climber can hang and lower their partner down).

FIGURE-OF-EIGHT LOOP

Although a bulkier knot, this is thought to be one of the most secure ways to create a loop in a rope, and has many uses.

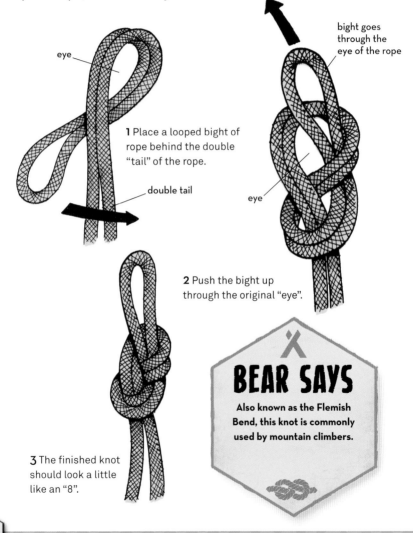

eye

1 Place a looped bight of rope behind the double "tail" of the rope.

double tail

bight goes through the eye of the rope

eye

2 Push the bight up through the original "eye".

3 The finished knot should look a little like an "8".

BEAR SAYS

Also known as the Flemish Bend, this knot is commonly used by mountain climbers.

THREADED FIGURE-OF-EIGHT

This should end up looking the same as the figure-of-eight loop knot, but it allows you to tie in to a fixed point, such as a harness or sling. It is done in two parts.

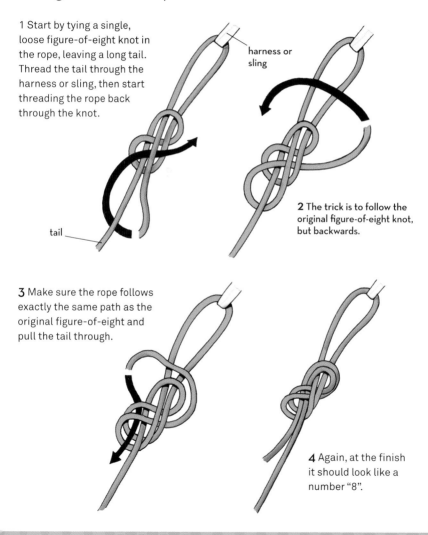

1 Start by tying a single, loose figure-of-eight knot in the rope, leaving a long tail. Thread the tail through the harness or sling, then start threading the rope back through the knot.

harness or sling

tail

2 The trick is to follow the original figure-of-eight knot, but backwards.

3 Make sure the rope follows exactly the same path as the original figure-of-eight and pull the tail through.

4 Again, at the finish it should look like a number "8".

JURY MAST KNOT

This knot can be used to "jury rig" (temporarily fix) a boat's mast if the existing rigging fails. The ropes holding the makeshift mast upright attach to the knot's three adjustable loops. A jury mast knot can also be used to put up a tent or flagpole, as long as there is something to prevent the knot sliding down.

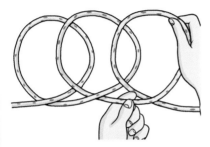

1 Working from left to right, make three underhand turns. The left edges of the second and third turns should overlap the right edges of the first and second turns.

BEAR SAYS

As well as being very useful, this knot is also attractive. It can be stitched to a bag or jacket sleeve for decoration.

2 Lead the left hand into the first turn from underneath, over the left edge of the second turn, under the right edge of the first turn, and pick up the left edge of the third.

3 With the right hand, lead over the right edge of the third turn, under the right edge of the second turn, over the left edge of the third turn, and pick up the right edge of the first.

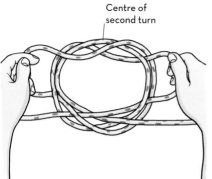

Centre of second turn

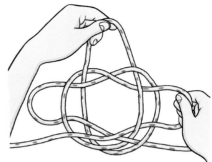

4 Draw your hands apart far enough so that two loose bights begin to form. The remainder of the knot should be circular in shape with an obvious hole in the middle.

5 The second turn is still in the circular portion of the knot. Draw it out carefully at the top to form a third bight. Adjust the knot so that the three bights are of a similar size.

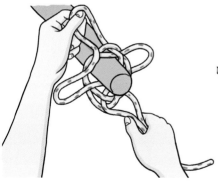

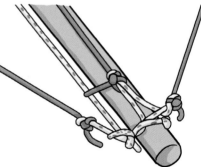

6 Place the knot over the end of a spar, and adjust to fit snugly. Tie both standing ends together around the spar. The three bights become attachment points for stays.

7 The stays – ropes or wires supporting the mast – can be attached to the jury mast knot with sheet bends or double sheet bends.

ANGLER'S LOOP

The angler's loop is a type of knot that forms a fixed, single loop, normally tied at the end of a rope. The angler's loop is difficult or impossible to untie, so it is best used where the line can be cut once the loop is no longer needed.

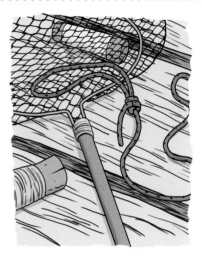

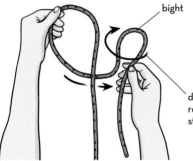

bight

direction of rotation in step two

1 Begin with a working part twice the length of the loop you wish to make. Make an underhand turn and then form a bight in the working end.

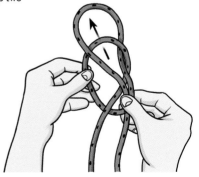

2 Rotate the bight right to left, then lead it through the turn from front to back. The bight will become the loop.

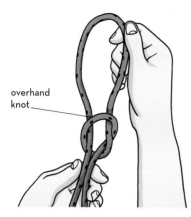

overhand knot

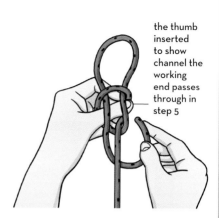

the thumb inserted to show channel the working end passes through in step 5

3 If the working end is too long, pull the extra cord into the loop. Work it out through the overhand knot and into the standing end.

4 Lead the working end around behind the standing part, next to the lower portion of the overhand knot.

in shock cord, work slack out in stages with fingers and tighten gradually. Shock cord will tend to stretch rather than slide through the knot

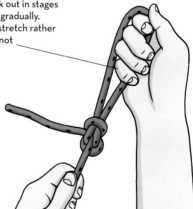

6 Tighten the knot by pulling on the loop, the standing part, and the working end. Pull hard on the loop and standing part to complete, particularly in shock cord, which stretches.

5 Slide the working end under both strands of the loop, from right to left.

BOTTLE SLING

This knot provides a carry handle for a bottle. It can be used to cool drinks in cold water slung over the side of a boat. This example requires about 1.5 m (5 ft) of cord.

> Binding knots are tied in a single piece of rope, around bundles of objects.

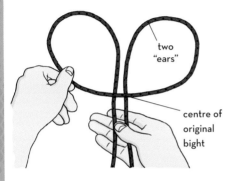

two "ears"

centre of original bight

1 Fold the rope in half, and place the bight flat on the table. Fold the bight down as shown, to make two even sized "ears".

BEAR SAYS

The bottle sling was used by ancient Greeks to carry jugs and bottles and also to make slings.

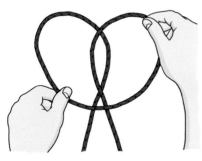

2 Slightly overlap the right ear over the left. The centre of the original bight should still be below the intersection of the two ears.

3 Holding the pattern in place on the table, draw the centre of the original bight under the knot at the point of the lower intersection of the ears.

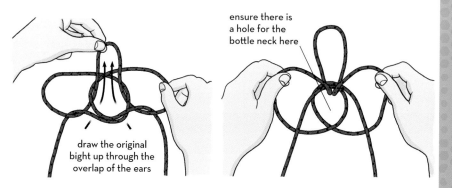

ensure there is
a hole for the
bottle neck here

draw the original
bight up through the
overlap of the ears

4 Now bring the centre of the original bight up through the space formed by the overlapping ears, to make a new bight at the top.

5 Using both hands, turn the ears and centre part over at the same time, with the top moving away from you. The top of the ears now finish at the bottom of the pattern.

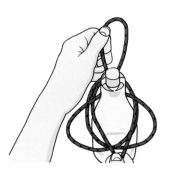

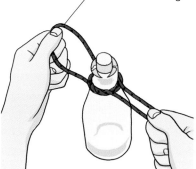

the ends can also be
tied to the bight to
form a handle or sling

6 Lift the knot carefully and place the hole over the neck of the bottle. Tighten by pulling on the upper bight and evenly on the pair of ends.

7 Work the knot to a snug fit around the neck of the bottle. The ends can be tied together to make a second handle, using a fisherman's knot or figure-of-eight bend.

ANCHOR BEND

The anchor bend, also known as the fisherman's bend, is quite a secure knot. It is most often finished by the addition of a half hitch. It will hold in bungee cord, whereas the "round turn and two half hitches" is particularly simple to tie, but it will not hold at all in bungee cord.

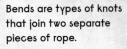

Bends are types of knots that join two separate pieces of rope.

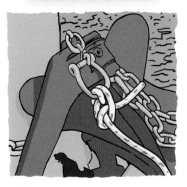

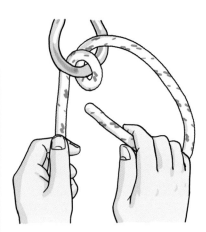

1 Make a round turn through a ring, winding from back to front and left to right. Do not pull the turn tight yet, as the working end needs to pass through it first.

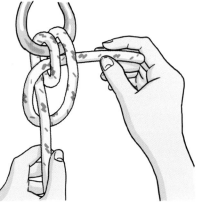

2 Lead the working end left behind the standing part, then to the front, and tuck it to the right beneath both windings of the round turn.

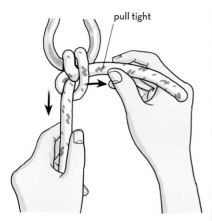

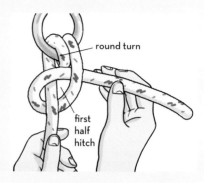

Round turn and two half hitches

3 Pull on both the standing part and working end to tighten the knot around the ring. This is a completed anchor bend, but a half hitch is usually added.

1 Make a round turn through the ring as in step one. Pass the working end around behind the standing part, to the front, and under itself, to make the first half hitch. Pull tight.

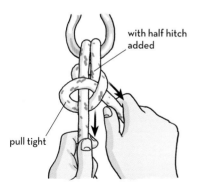

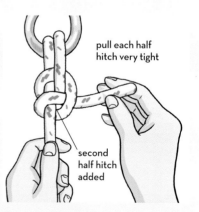

4 Pass the working end around behind the standing part again, to the front, and under itself. Pull the working end as tight as possible.

2 Continue the working end in the same direction, around behind the standing part and to the front again, and make the second half hitch.

DOUBLE FISHERMAN'S KNOT

This is one of the best knots to safely tie two ropes together, and is useful on long descents. Start by laying the last metre (3 ft) of each rope alongside each other, tails in opposite directions.

1 Turn the end of one rope around the other rope twice, and pass the end back through the loops, away from the knot's centre. Do this to both ropes.

rope two

two turns

rope one

2 This should form two "x" shapes, which will then slide together as you pull each rope.

pull each rope to finish

PRUSIK HITCH

The prusik knot is an excellent way to attach a weight to a rope. It slides up and down the rope when unweighted, but doesn't slip under a downward force. Two prusik knots (one for your feet, one clipped into the harness) are often used to climb up, or "prusik", a rope.

Hitches are used to attach load-bearing cordage to objects. The choice of hitch is important if the knot needs to remain secure.

prusik cord must have a smaller diameter than the main rope

1 Wrap the loop around the rope, and back through itself.

2 Repeat this process twice more so there is a triple loop top and bottom.

3 Push the knot together. It will slide up, but will hold if force is applied downwards.

CLOVE HITCHES

The clove hitch is a quick and memorable knot that can be used to attach a rope to a pole or a carabiner. It may slip on a smooth surface. The load can be applied to either end of the rope. Steps one and two show the clove hitch tied with a working end. The alternate "in-the-hand" method allows the hitch to be tied in the bight – anywhere along the rope.

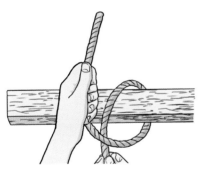

1 Lead the working end over and down behind the pole, then up in front and over itself to the left.

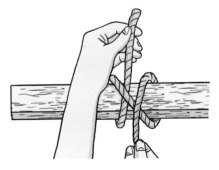

2 Lead the working end diagonally across the turn, around the back of the rail again, then upwards under itself. You have formed two half hitches. Pull the ends to tighten.

Alternate clove hitch

This method can be used when you can slip the hitch over the end of a pole.

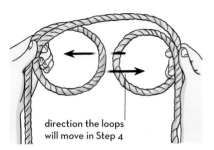

direction the loops will move in Step 4

left turn sitting over right

1 If you don't have easy access to the ends of the rope, tie the clove hitch using this alternate method. Begin by making two consecutive overhand turns.

2 Slide the left-hand turn over the right, then slide the fingers of the left hand through the centre of both loops.

3 When viewed from the side, the two half hitches can be identified. It is the same knot as shown in step two of the simpler clove hitch, shown to the left.

4 Simply slide the half hitches over the end of the pole and tighten.

Clove hitch for a carabiner

This hitch is also used in climbing. It can be used to safely lower climbing gear from a great height. It increases the amount of friction on the rope but also allows it to slip, so it can be used instead of a belay.

1 Make two loops in the rope, both in the same direction.

2 Place the lower loop over the higher loop, so that both tails of the rope are in the middle of the hitch.

lower loop

higher loop

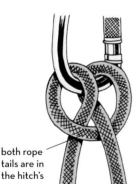

both rope tails are in the hitch's centre

3 Clip a carabiner through the two loops. The hitch is surprisingly strong.

22

ITALIAN HITCH

This hitch can be used to safely lower climbing gear from a great height. It increases the amount of friction on the rope but also allows it to slip, so it can be used instead of a belay.

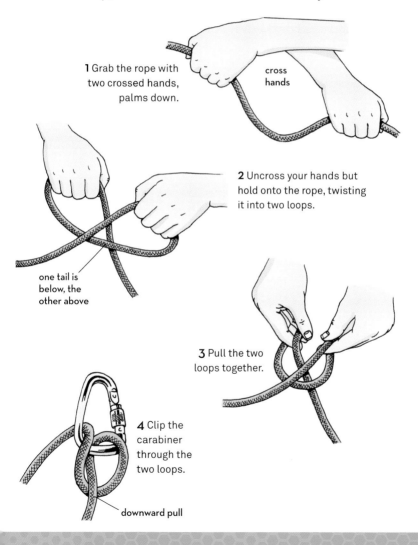

1 Grab the rope with two crossed hands, palms down.

cross hands

2 Uncross your hands but hold onto the rope, twisting it into two loops.

one tail is below, the other above

3 Pull the two loops together.

4 Clip the carabiner through the two loops.

downward pull

PILE HITCH

Pile hitches can be used to attach a dinghy to a post, or an anchor line to a bollard. They can be tied in the bight or at the end of a rope. The length of the working end required to tie the hitch will depend on the thickness of the post. To untie, ease some of the working end back into the hitch until there is enough slack to lift the bight off the top of the post.

BEAR SAYS

Make sure there isn't tension on the other end of the rope while tying this hitch.

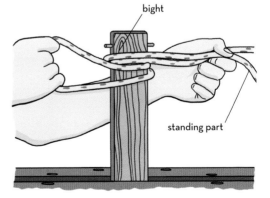

bight

standing part

1 Form a bight long enough to pass several times around the post. Hold the standing parts in one hand. With the other, wrap the bight around the post, underneath both standing parts.

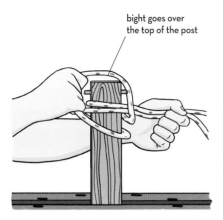

bight goes over the top of the post

2 Widen the bight and place it over the top of the post.

Double pile hitch

The double pile hitch is very secure but a little more complicated to untie.

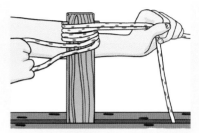

1 Complete step one of the pile hitch (shown left), then wind the bight around the post a second time, before placing it over the post. The second winding is made lower down the post than the first.

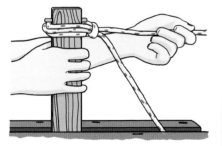

3 Pull evenly on both ends to firm the hitch. If the rope is sticking and not tightening evenly around the post, you may have to help it, but be careful not to catch your fingers.

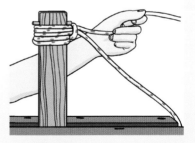

2 Adjust the hitch as in step three of the pile hitch. With both hitches, make sure that you hold the ends together until the bight is placed over the post, so that both ends are secure.

HIGHWAYMAN'S HITCH

The highwayman's hitch is a useful knot to know because it instantly releases with a tug on the working end. However, it is not the most secure of hitches can be loosened quite easily.

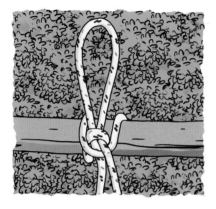

BEAR SAYS

The highwayman's hitch isn't secure enough for use in climbing or mountaineering.

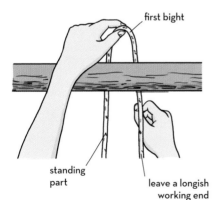

first bight

standing part

leave a longish working end

1 Form a long bight in the left hand, with the working end to the right of the standing part, and lead it up behind the rail.

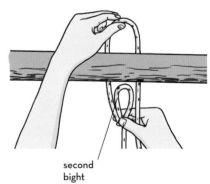

second bight

2 With the right hand, form a second bight in the standing part, with the remainder of the standing part on the right side of this new bight.

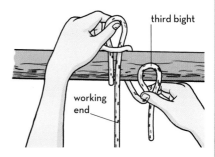

second bight
led into first

third bight

working
end

working
end

standing
part

3 Tuck this second bight up through the first, hold it in place with your left hand, and tighten the first bight around the second by pulling on the working end.

4 With the right hand, form a third bight in the working part, with the working end to the right.

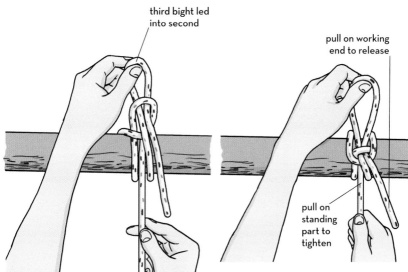

third bight led
into second

pull on working
end to release

pull on
standing
part to
tighten

5 Lead this third bight fully up into the second, so that there is no slack around the rail.

6 Pull on the standing part to firm the second bight around the third. To release, pull on the working end and the hitch will slide apart.

TIMBER HITCH

The timber hitch is an easy method of securing a rope to a pole. With the timber hitch tied at the centre of gravity, the pole can be hoisted up. The addition of a half hitch forms the killick hitch, which allows the pole to be towed on land or through water. The timber hitch is also used to attach nylon strings to a guitar bridge.

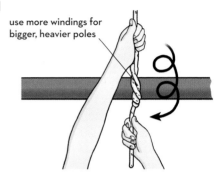

use more windings for bigger, heavier poles

2 Wind the working end around the turn again once, twice, or three times. Pull tight on the standing part and ease the slack out of the windings through the working end.

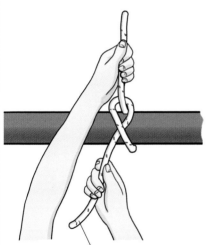

alternatively, go over the turn first, then under it from left to right

1 Make a loose turn around the pole from the back to the front. Pass the working end behind the standing part, to the front, and under the turn.

Killick hitch

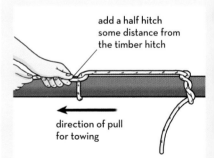

add a half hitch some distance from the timber hitch

direction of pull for towing

3 Lead the standing part along the pole and tie a half hitch. Tying it nearer the end provides better stability when towing, but too near the end and it will slip off.

ROLLING HITCH

The rolling hitch is used to tie a rope to a pole or to larger rope, when the load is to be applied at an angle between 45 and 90 degrees to the pole. The direction of the load, or strain, will decide the way in which the knot must be tied. The hitches shown here take the strain from the right.

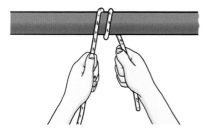

1 Begin the hitch with a round turn, going up and over, and from left to right.

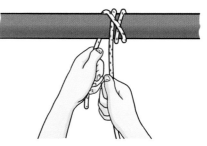

2 Pass the working end diagonally left across both windings, then down around the back of the pole.

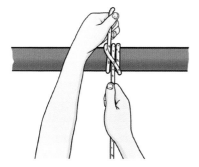

3 Tuck the working end up under the diagonal. Note that the rolling hitch is actually a clove hitch with an extra turn around the pole on the right.

BEAR SAYS

The tautline hitch is similar to the rolling hitch, and is suitable for attaching a line to a taut rope.

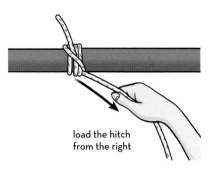

load the hitch
from the right

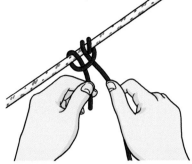

4 Pull both ends to tighten. The load can be applied from the right of the hitch. For loading from the left, begin tying the hitch as in step one, but winding from right to left.

5 Lead the working end up behind the rope, to the front, and tuck it under itself, parallel to the standing part. The knot looks like a cow hitch with an extra turn.

Tautline hitch

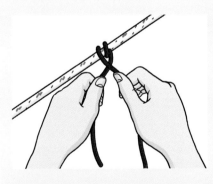

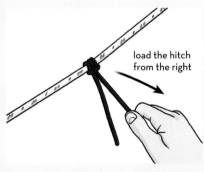

load the hitch
from the right

1 Tie this hitch using a line that is at least half the diameter of the taut rope. Complete step one of the rolling hitch, then lead the working end left in front of the standing part.

2 Pull both ends to firm the hitch tight around the rope. As with the rolling hitch, the strain can be applied from the direction in which the initial overhand turn was made.

TRUCKER'S HITCH

As it can be tensioned further after tightening, this knot is suitable for tying tent stays, or securing a load on a trailer. The hitch provides leverage, allowing the rope to be pulled tight, and uses up any excess cordage.

BEAR SAYS

The trucker's hitch is also known as the waggoner's hitch or dolly knot.

this knot requires a length of rope four to five times the distance from the hitch's starting point to the securing point

1 Begin with the standing part tied to an upper fastening point. Rotating counterclockwise, make a small overhand turn and secure it in your left hand.

2 With your right hand, form a bight in the working part. It will need to have a length approximately half the distance from the turn to the securing point.

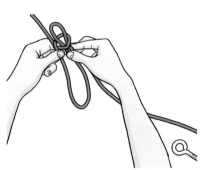

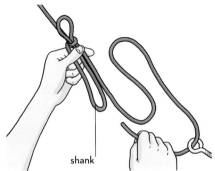

shank

3 Lead the end of the bight into the overhand turn from below – not too far in, about a fifth of its length will do. Secure the bight and overhand turn in your left hand.

4 This forms a new, lower bight, called a shank. Lead the working end down and through the lower fastening point.

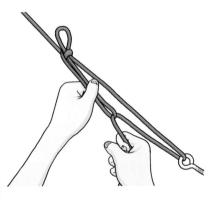

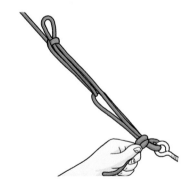

5 Lead the working end up through the shank from back to front. Apply downward tension to the working end. The turn will grip the bight and you can let go with the left hand.

6 Pull the end as tight as necessary and tie it off above the fastening point – a couple of half hitches should do. The trucker's hitch requires some practice to master.

SQUARE LASHING

Square lashing is a relatively easy way to secure two poles at right angles. Be careful with the tension and the number of windings – the lashing must be strong enough for the job, but not so tight that the poles are bent.

> Lashing is a method of fastening items together with cord. They are permanent and use multiple windings.

later additional windings will lock the tail securely.

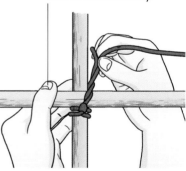

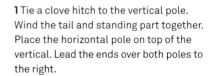

BEAR SAYS

To join poles together, lashings are used. They can be useful around campsites to help build chairs and tables.

1 Tie a clove hitch to the vertical pole. Wind the tail and standing part together. Place the horizontal pole on top of the vertical. Lead the ends over both poles to the right.

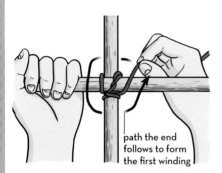

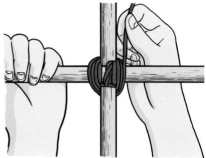

path the end
follows to form
the first winding

2 Maintaining the tension, lead the cord behind the upper vertical pole, over and down in front of the left horizontal pole, around behind the lower vertical pole and to the front.

3 Repeat the winding process about four times. The number of windings will depend on the diameter of the poles and the thickness of the cord.

frapping turns do not bind pole to pole but compress the existing windings

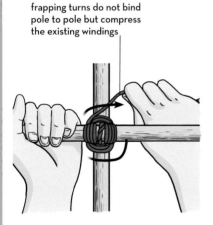

clove hitch to finish

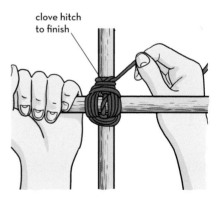

4 Start the frapping turns. Make a turn over the right horizontal pole, then wind clockwise between the two poles three or four times.

5 Stop at the top left and tie a tight clove hitch around the upper vertical pole, so the lashing can't slide or rotate under tension.

DIAGONAL LASHING

Diagonal lashing is used to secure poles that cross diagonally together. The two poles don't have to be at right angles — the timber hitch at the start pulls both poles together without changing their position. However, if the poles are not held in place, the angle can be difficult to keep during lashing.

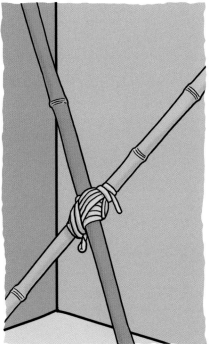

lead the cord away from you and around the back

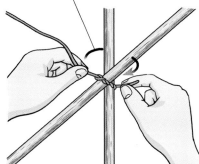

1 Tie a timber hitch around both poles, at the intersection with the widest angle. Tighten the hitch and lead the cord away from you, around the back of both poles.

the tension applied in the diagonal lashing process isn't as great as in square lashing, but there is less chance of the poles sliding

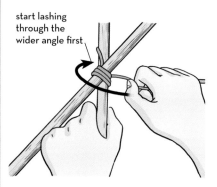

start lashing through the wider angle first

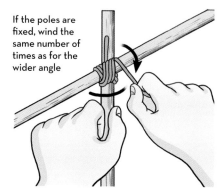

If the poles are fixed, wind the same number of times as for the wider angle

2 Wind tightly over the top of the hitch and around the middle four or five times. Unless the poles are fixed, the tighter you wind, the wider the angle becomes.

3 Now wind across the other, narrower angle. If the poles are not fixed, apply pressure and continue winding until you achieve the angle you want.

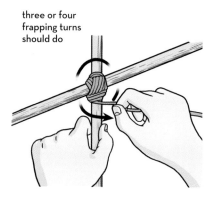

three or four frapping turns should do

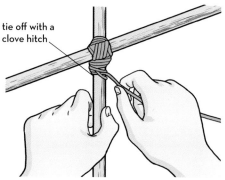

tie off with a clove hitch

4 Wind the cord counterclockwise by passing in front of the upper vertical pole, behind the left cross pole, in front of the lower vertical pole and behind the right cross pole.

5 Finish with a clove hitch around one of the poles. Line it up with the end of the frapping turns so that there is little chance of the hitch sliding or rotating under tension.

SHEAR LASHING

A shear lashing can secure two poles together to reinforce them. It can also extend a pole if the lashing is placed near the end, at the point where the two poles overlap. Tied a little more loosely, it makes an A-frame lashing. Here, the two poles are separated slightly so that they can be moved apart. The A-frame is also known as shear legs and can be used for a tent or lean-to shelter.

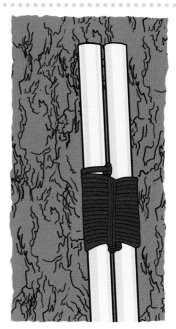

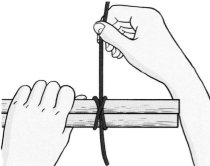

1 Lay two poles side by side and tie together with a clove hitch. Leave the shorter end long enough to be secured underneath the windings.

cover the short end of the clove hitch with the lashing

2 Begin winding, but not as tightly for an A-frame as for securing two poles. As a rule, make the binding length no less than the width of the two poles.

cover the short end
of the clove hitch
with the lashing

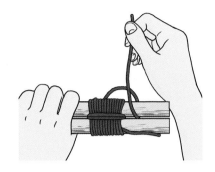

3 For the frapping turns, lead the cord behind the top pole and to the front between the poles. Wind across the existing windings, between the poles.

4 Finish at the opposite end to the original clove hitch and tie another clove hitch around one pole, not both. The hitch must be tight, and snug against the lashing.

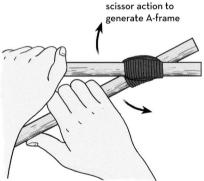

scissor action to
generate A-frame

5 If tying poles together to reinforce or extend them, make a tighter binding, leave out the frapping turns, and finish with a clove hitch around both poles.

6 To use as an A-frame, separate the poles by using a scissor action, stretching the cord equally at both ends of the lashing. Practice will help you apply the right lashing tension.

TRIPOD LASHING

There are different methods of tying tripod lashings but this one can be tied into a frame, taken to a site, and put up. After use it can be folded flat and taken away, with a temporary binding (such as the pole lashing) securing the other end. However, it doesn't form the perfect triangle shape at its base. Like the shear lashing, the angle at which the legs can be separated depends on the length and tension of the lashing, and the stretch in the cord.

when beginning, leave space for the width of the lashing plus enough space to hang an item

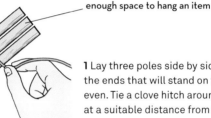

1 Lay three poles side by side, making sure the ends that will stand on the ground are even. Tie a clove hitch around the top pole at a suitable distance from the ends.

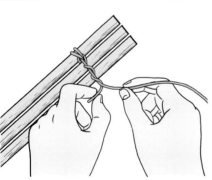

2 Wind the short clove hitch end around the working end and lead both ends towards you across the three poles. This will help lock the clove hitch and its tail.

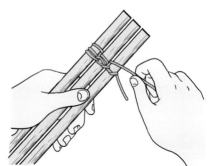

3 Start winding between the poles: under the bottom pole, over the centre, under the top, then around and over, this time under the centre pole, and over the bottom.

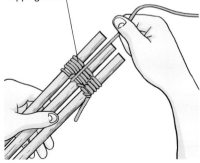

wind for about the width of two poles. Stop with the cord coming from behind the top pole. Begin frapping turns

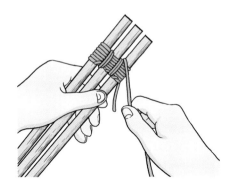

4 Begin frapping turns by leading the cord down in front of the top pole, then to the back between the top and centre poles. Form two or three turns around the windings.

5 Lead the cord behind the centre pole, and to the front between the centre and bottom poles. Make a second set of frapping turns in the opposite direction to the first.

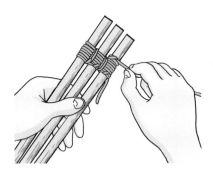

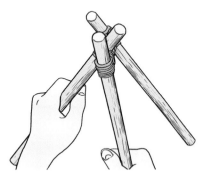

6 To finish, tie off with a clove hitch around the bottom pole. The frapping turn must lead straight into the hitch so that there is no chance of it rotating.

7 To erect the tripod, separate the outer poles and use a scissor action to swing the centre pole in the opposite direction. This may be difficult if the lashing is too tight.

EYE SPLICE

Rope splicing is a way of joining two pieces of rope by unravelling their strands and then weaving them together. A splice is used where a rope is fixed permanently to an item or slipped over a hook, stake, or bollard. An eye splice isn't actually a knot, but a way to form an "eye" in the end of a length of laid rope.

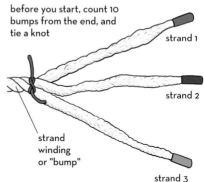

before you start, count 10 bumps from the end, and tie a knot

strand 1

strand 2

strand winding or "bump"

strand 3

> Splicing is a traditional method used to permanently join two laid ropes.

1 Begin to unlay the rope. As you separate the strands, bind them with tape. Continue to unlay the strands up to the knot. Number each strand.

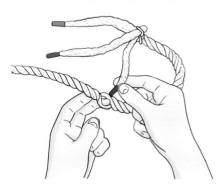

2 Open the lay of the rope to raise one strand. Feed the central strand, strand 2, diagonally left under the raised strand in the standing part. Do not pull it through completely yet.

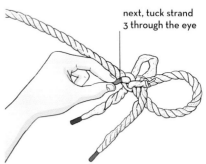

next, tuck strand 3 through the eye

3 Feed strand 3, which is to the right of strand 2, under its corresponding right strand in the standing part, that is, the strand to the right of the one that strand 2 is tucked under.

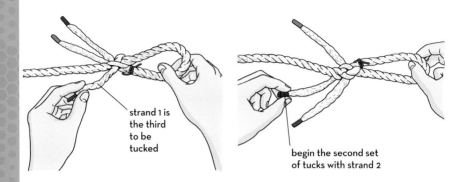

strand 1 is
the third
to be
tucked

begin the second set
of tucks with strand 2

4 Rotate the rope slightly, and tuck the remaining strand 1 under its corresponding left strand of the standing part. Pull the three unlaid strands snugly up to the standing part.

5 Continue weaving the unlaid strands in this diagonal pattern until you have completed four sets of tucks. Three may be enough, but not if the lay of the rope is loose.

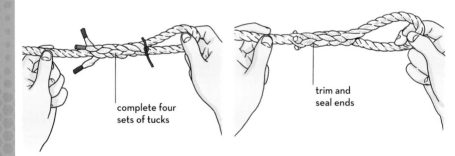

complete four
sets of tucks

trim and
seal ends

6 Maintain the even twist in the unlaid strands as you tuck. If you don't open the lay in the standing part sufficiently, the twist in the strands will increase as you go.

7 Thick rope may need the assistance of a fid (a cone-shaped tool) for opening the lay. After the fourth tuck, the ends can be trimmed and either sealed with heat or whipped (binded with twine).

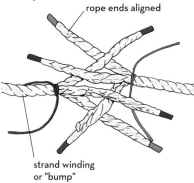

SHORT SPLICE

This is a method of permanently joining two lengths of laid rope of a similar thickness. This method avoids the rope becoming thicker at the join.

rope ends aligned

strand winding or "bump"

BEAR SAYS

Although it looks complicated, if you colour code the strands, the technique becomes far simpler.

1 Tie a constrictor knot around each piece of rope about 12 bumps from the end. Tape and number the strands and unwind them. Align the strands of the rope ends.

begin tucking the left rope into the right

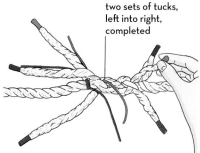

two sets of tucks, left into right, completed

2 Following steps two to four of the eye splice (p.41), begin to weave the left rope into the right. Make two sets of tucks.

3 Make a set of tucks of the right rope into the left. Tighten the strands and adjust the alignment of one rope to the other. Loosen the constrictor knots as needed.

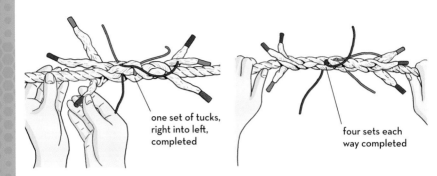

one set of tucks,
right into left,
completed

four sets each
way completed

4 Make another set of tucks with the right rope into the left, so that there are two sets in each direction. Then make alternate sets until you have four in each direction.

5 The splice is completed and the ends can be trimmed and sealed. However, if you wish to taper the splice so that it blends neatly into the rest of the rope, proceed to step six.

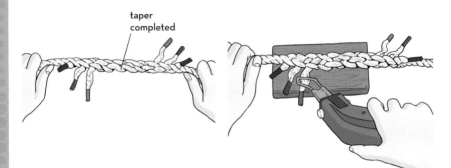

taper
completed

6 An easy way to taper is to not tuck one strand of each set after three tucks, leave out a second strand after the fourth tuck, and make a fifth tuck with the one remaining strand.

7 When the tucking of each strand is completed in the correct order, the splice will have an even taper. Trim and seal the ends neatly.

IMPOSSIBLE KNOT

Put a length of rope in front of your friends and challenge them to pick it up then tie a knot without letting go with either hand. The result must be a proper knot that does not collapse when the rope is pulled tight.

BEAR SAYS

The trick behind mastering the impossible knot is plenty of practice, so you can demonstrate it quickly!

1 Lay the rope on a table. Before picking it up, cross your arms over each other. Now lean over and pick up one end of the rope in each hand.

Rope tricks are ways of tying and untying a knot that at first glance appear impossible!

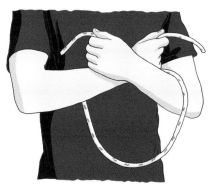

2 Keeping a firm hold on the rope, uncross your arms and move your hands apart, letting the rope slip over your wrists and hands as you do so.

3 With this trick, you tie an overhand knot in the rope without letting go of either end.

RING DROP

This trick allows you to remove a ring that has been threaded onto a loop. The loop should be made from a length of thin cord about one metre (3 ft) long. Practise this first so you know how to do it quickly, then amaze your friends by getting them to try first – then if they can't figure it out, show them how it is done!

1 With the loop hanging over both your thumbs, hook the right little finger around the upper strand, to the left of the ring and from behind.

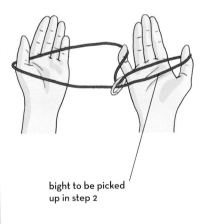

bight to be picked up in step 2

2 With your left little finger, reach over the bight formed by the right little finger, and hook it around the upper strand to the right of the ring, again from behind.

let the loop slide off the left little finger in step 3

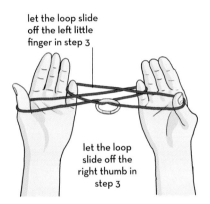

let the loop slide off the right thumb in step 3

3 To free the ring, move your hands apart while letting the loop slip off the left little finger and the right thumb.

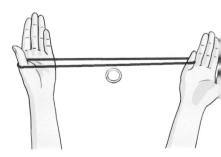

NOT A KNOT

This trick, which begins with a reef knot, looks very complicated, but the knot falls apart completely when pulled tight. The final step is easiest to carry out if thin cord or flexible rope is used rather than thick or stiff rope. A piece of cord about one metre (3 ft) long is ideal.

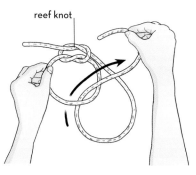

reef knot

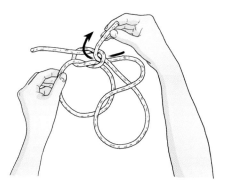

1 Form a loop and tie a reef knot. Pick up the working end that emerges towards the back of the knot and lead it through the loop from back to front.

2 Lead the same working end through the centre of the reef knot, again from back to front.

BEAR SAYS

Once you have mastered the puzzle, give a reef knot to your friends and challenge them to make it collapse without untying it.

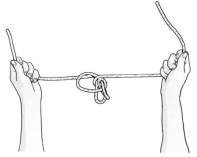

3 Pull firmly on both ends of the cord. The original reef knot will collapse and disappear completely.

Discover more amazing books in the Bear Grylls series:

Perfect for young adventurers, the *Survival Skills* series accompanies an exciting range of colouring and activity books. Curious kids can also learn tips and tricks for almost any extreme situation in *Survival Camp*, and explore Earth in *Extreme Planet*.

Conceived by Weldon Owen in partnership
with Bear Grylls Ventures

Produced by Weldon Owen Ltd
Suite 3.08 The Plaza, 535 King's Road,
London SW10 0SZ, UK

WELDON OWEN LTD
Publisher Donna Gregory
Designer Shahid Mahmood
Editorial Claire Philip and Sophia Podini
Illustrators Peter Bull Studios (original illustrations),
Bernard Chau (colour)

Printed in Malaysia

10 9 8 7 6 5 4 3 2 1

Disclaimer
Weldon Owen and Bear Grylls take pride in doing our best to get the facts right in putting together the information in this book, but occasionally something slips past our beady eyes. Therefore we make no warranties about the accuracy or completeness of the information in the book and to the maximum extent permitted, we disclaim all liability. Wherever possible, we will endeavour to correct any errors of fact at reprint.

Kids – if you want to try any of the activities in this book, please ask your parents first! Parents – all outdoor activities carry some degree of risk and we recommend that anyone participating in these activities be aware of the risks involved and seek professional instruction and guidance. None of the health/medical information in this book is intended as a substitute for professional medical advice; always seek the advice of a qualified practitioner.

A WELDON OWEN PRODUCTION.
PART OF THE BONNIER PUBLISHING GROUP.